my soul shall speak

Alyssa Orians

BookLeaf
Publishing

India | USA | UK

Presentation by *BookLeaf Publishing*

Web: www.bookleafpub.com

E-mail: info@bookleafpub.com

ISBN: 978-93-5744-359-3

First edition 2022

DEDICATION

In memory of my father, Kim Orians. You have my love always.

I

1

Find me in the darkness -A. Orians

II

2

Will you save me when I am lost in my head? -
A. Orians

III

3

Save me when I am drowning. When I am deep below the surface, struggling for air. My eyes will find you, pleading. Saying, "please save me." Jump in and rescue me, for I am too young to die. - A. Orians

IV

4

Today's the day. The day we climb out of this whole we've dug. Take my hand, just one step at a time. Don't look back -A. Orians

V

My heart aches without you -A. Orians

VI

6

These dreams seem so real, but the nightmare begins when I wake up. Empty. Take me with you while I sleep, for I do not wish to be here alone much longer. -A. Orians

VII

7

I will no longer waste time on people who do
not make time for me -A. Orians

VIII

My heart yearns for you, for your voice, your touch. How do I tell my heart to yearn no more? For you are gone. -A. Orians

IX

I hope you are happy now. I hope Heaven is
wonderful as it sounds. -A Orians

X

I cannot bear the thought of living without you. -
A. Orians

XI

The world without you is a cold, dark place. The walls are crashing down, I cannot hold them up much longer. The world I once knew is caving around me. - A. Orians

XII

12

Who will I run to when you leave me? Who do I turn to for support? What do I do when I need you and you are not there? - A. Orians

XIII

13

I am lonely without you. - A. Orians

XIV

14

What would it take for Heaven to let you come back? To realize they took one too soon? I wish I could call Heaven and talk to you. - A. Orians

XV

You left me when I needed you the most. You hurt me and now you want to come back. It's too late now, I'm broken and damaged. You left me empty and pushed me away. Why would I let down the walls that I built piece by piece after you left, just to have them torn down again? - A. Orians

XVI

It's funny how people change. One minute they love you, the next they won't even be there for you in the worst parts of your life. - A. Orians

XVII

17

You took a piece of me that will never be
replaced. You hurt me so deeply that I don't
know how to trust again. My best friend, my
closest companion. You left me for another girl
and hurt my heart in the process. You left our
friendship and told me you never wanted to talk
again. All for the 9 months of "love" you
wanted. - A. Orians

XVII

18

Darling, trust is a fragile thing. You can spend a lifetime trying to earn someone's trust, but destroy trust in a second. The second you lose trust, you also lose your chance at getting it back. - A. Orians

XIX

19

I miss you. - A. Orians

XX

I hope you're happy now. - A. Orians